What Do I See?

by Wiley Blevins
illustrated by Christiane Engel

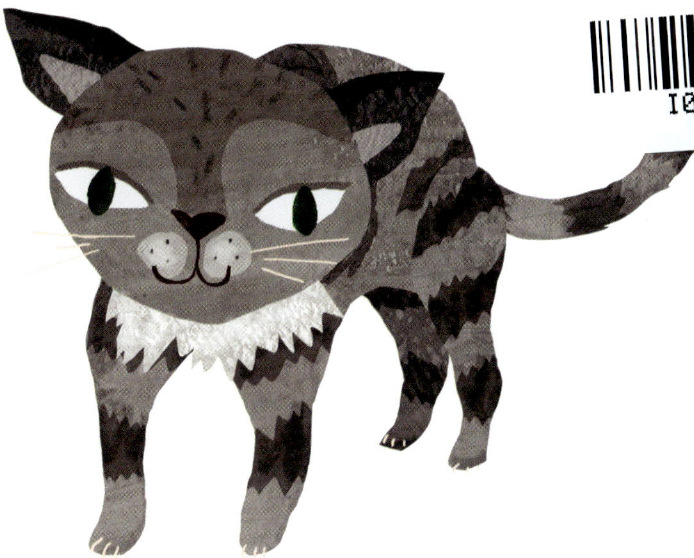

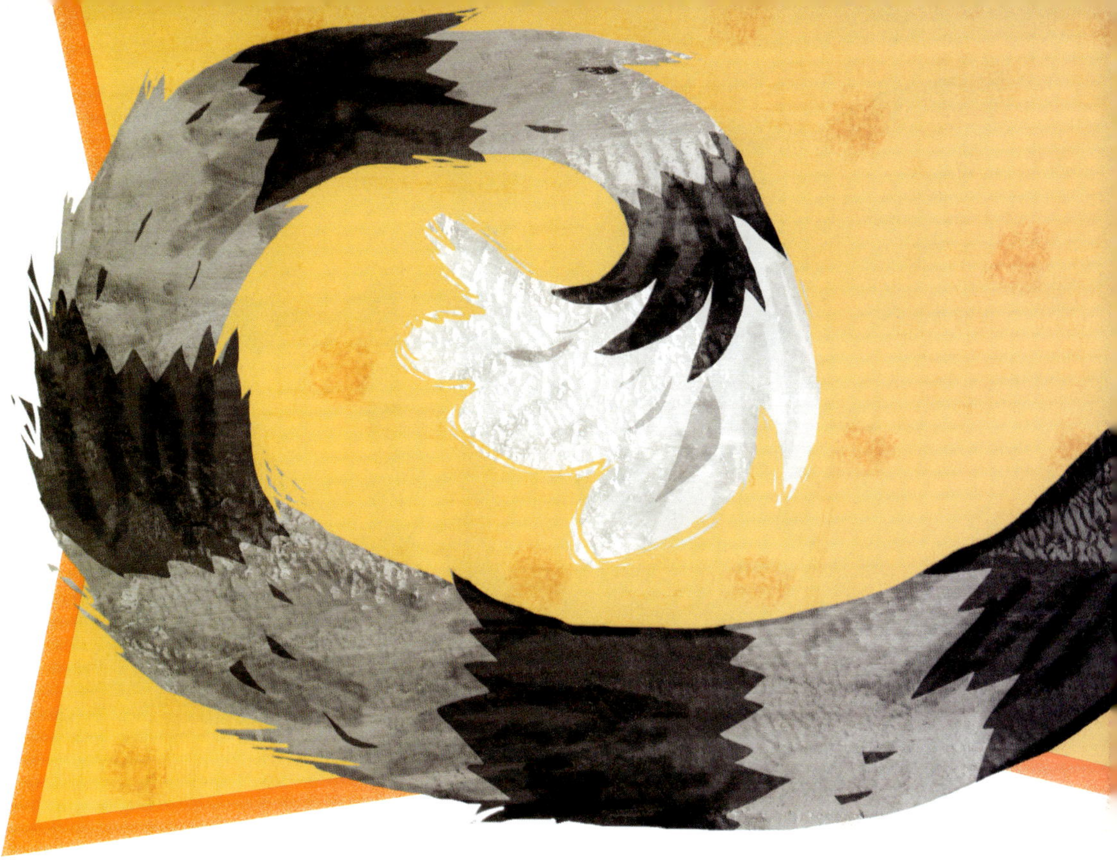

I see a tail.

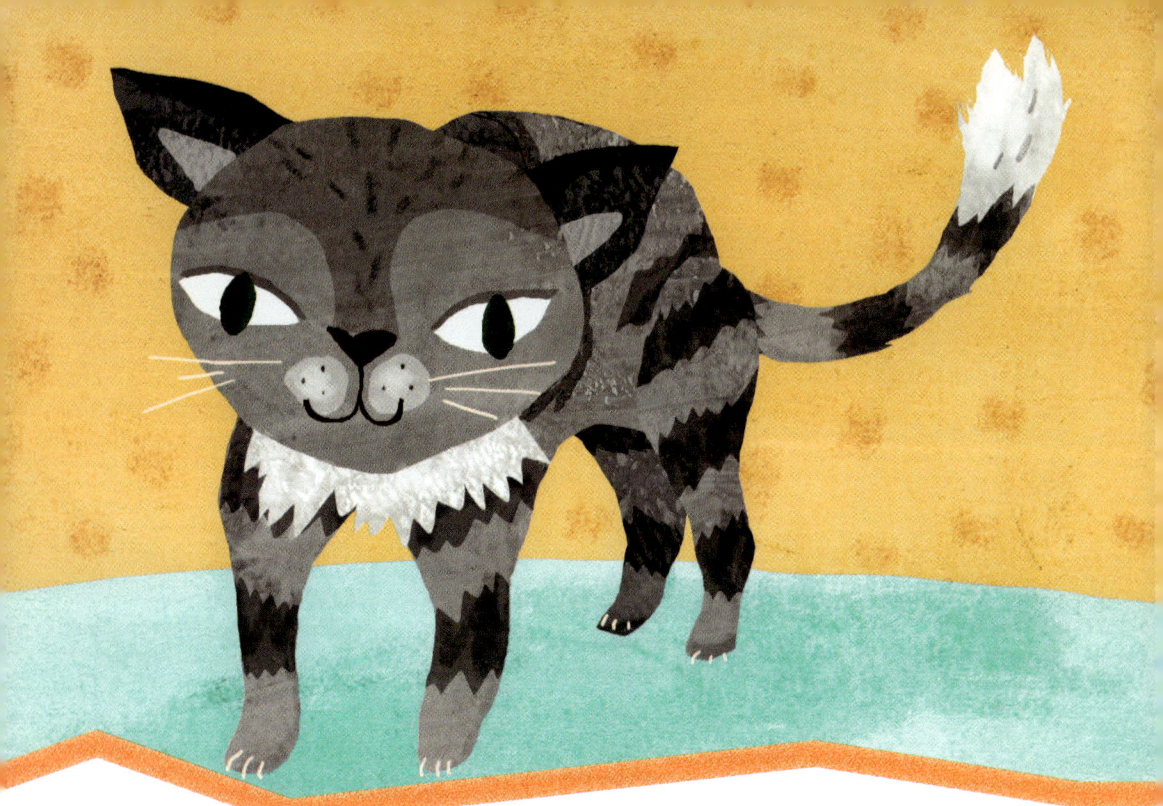

I see a cat.

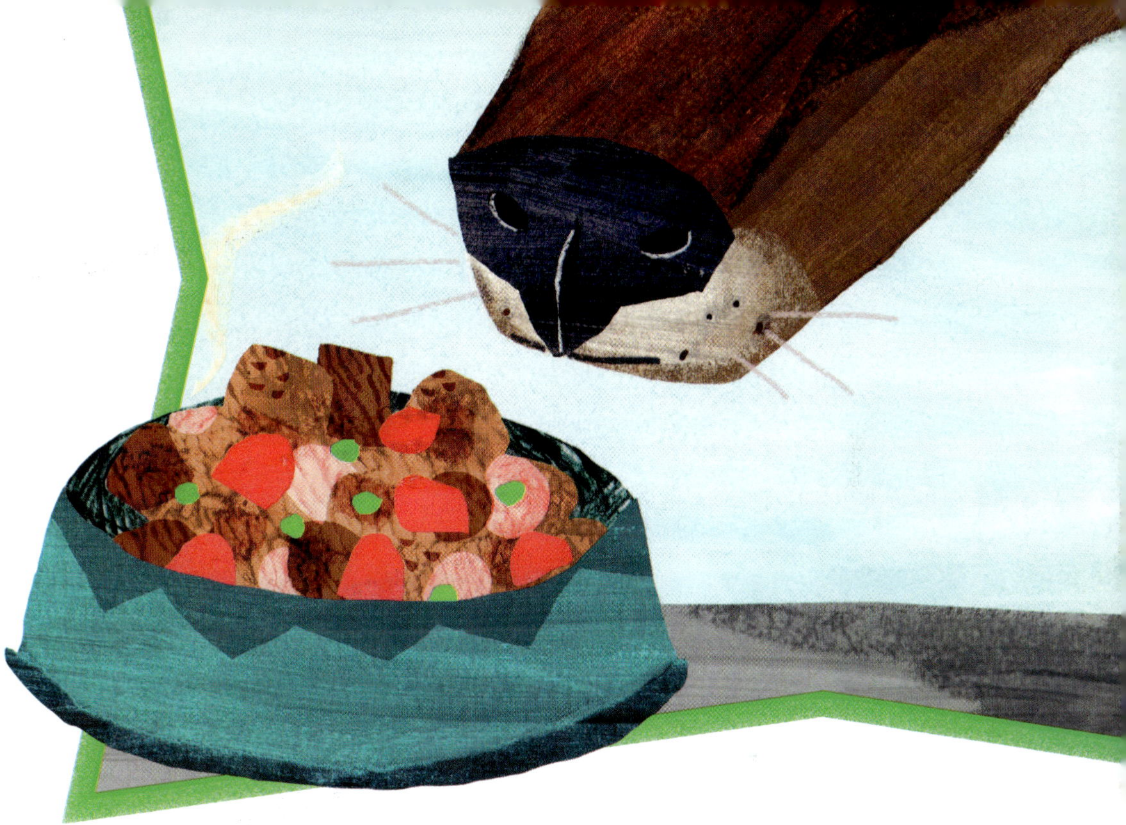

I see a nose.

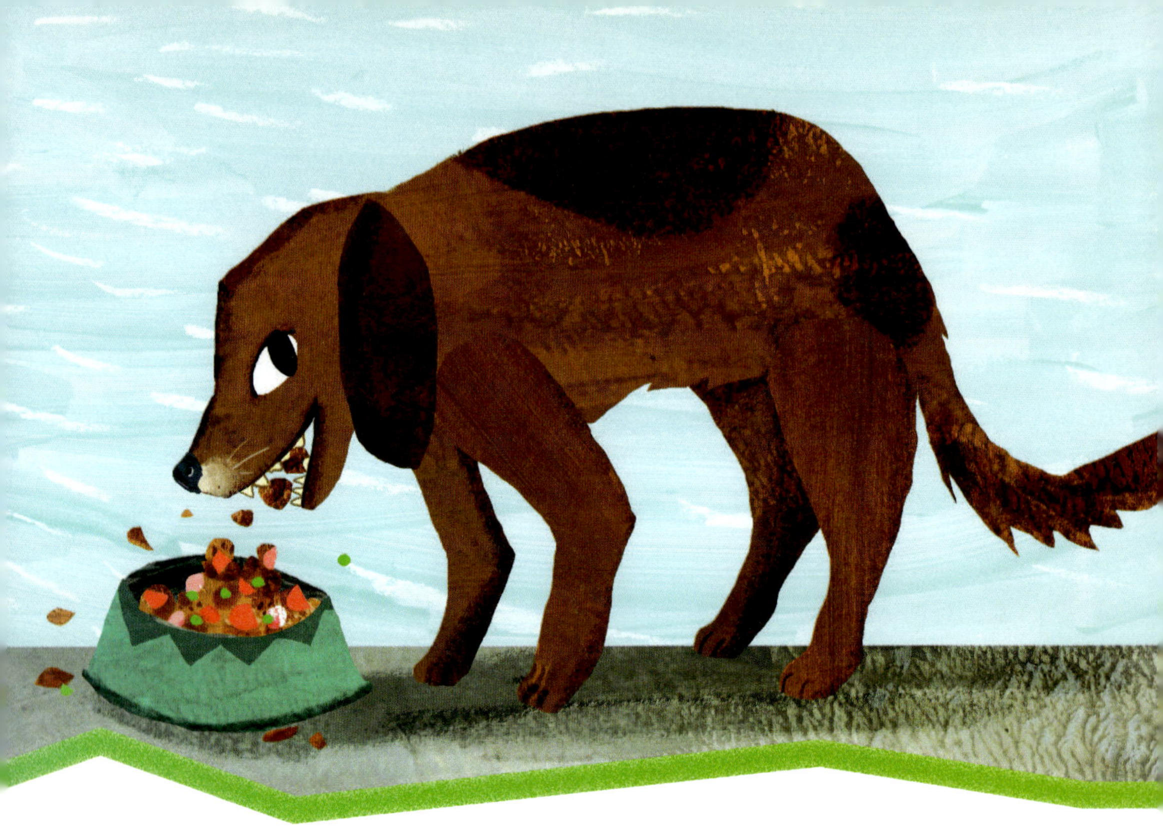

I see a dog.

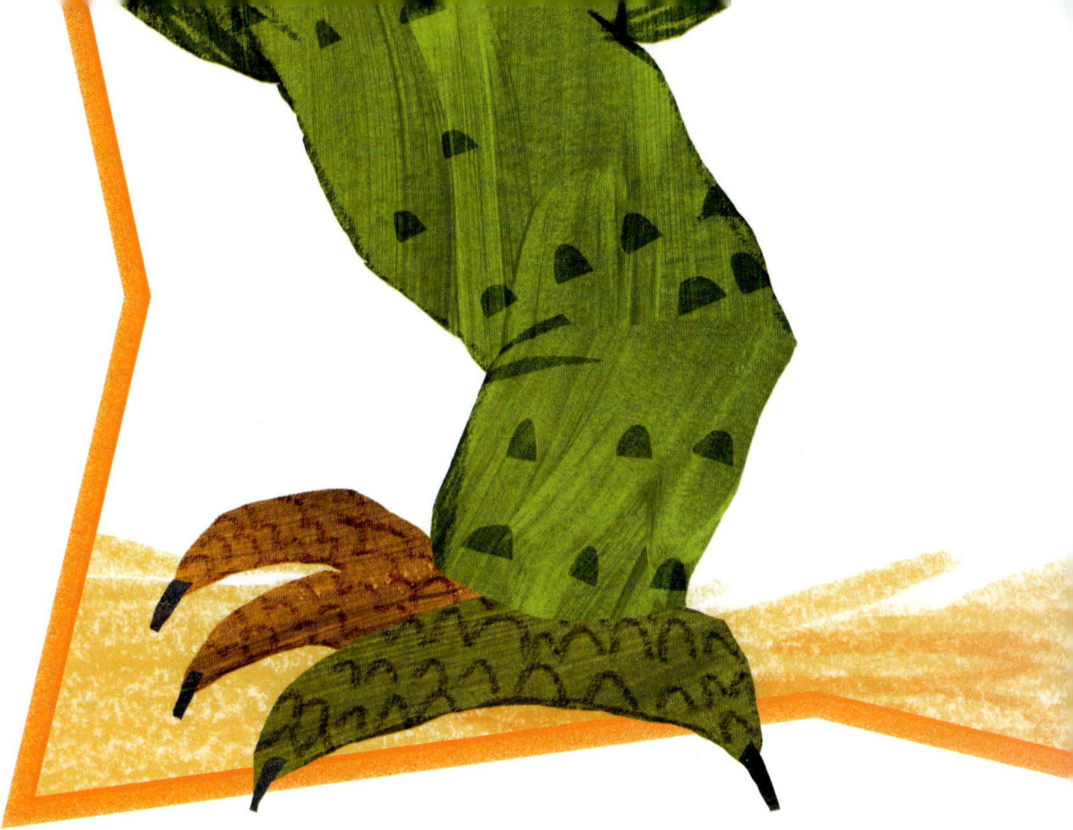

I see a foot.

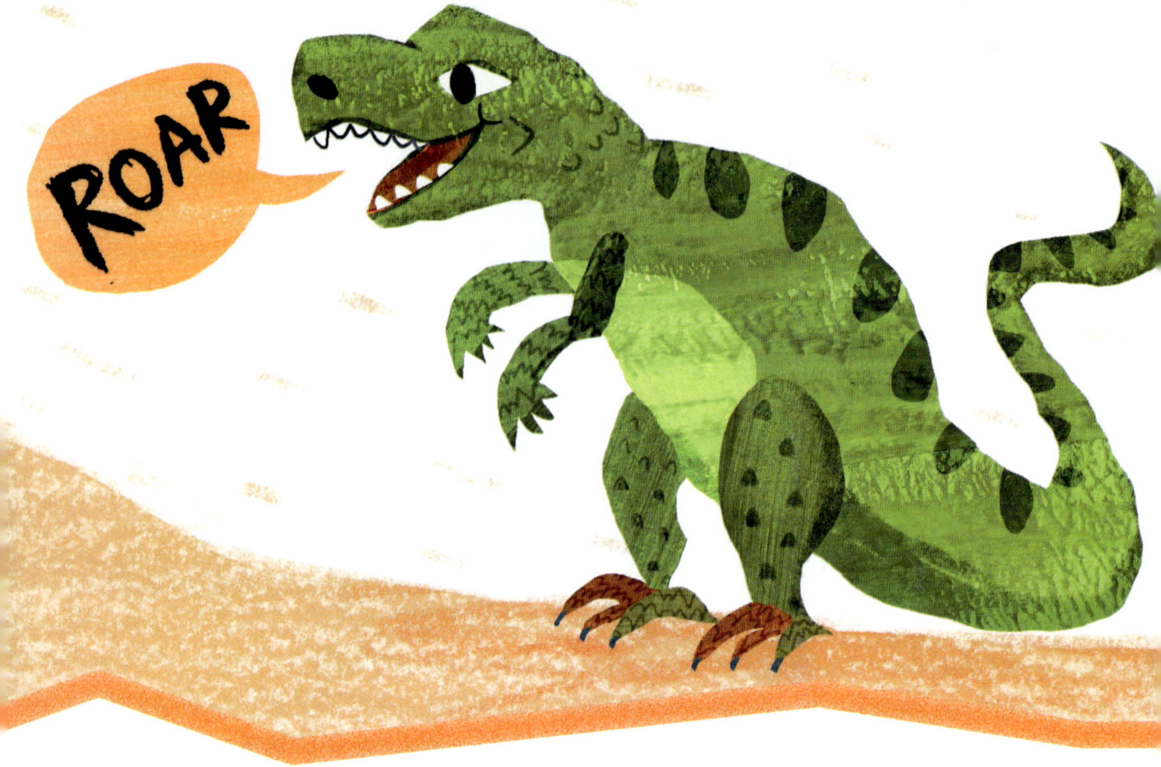

I see a dinosaur!